THE THRESHOLD
OF THE NEW

Publication of this book was supported by a grant from the Eric Mathieu King Fund of The Academy of American Poets.

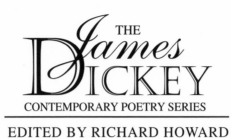

THE
James
DICKEY
CONTEMPORARY POETRY SERIES

EDITED BY RICHARD HOWARD

THE THRESHOLD
OF THE NEW

Poems by Henry Sloss

UNIVERSITY OF SOUTH CAROLINA PRESS

© 1997 Henry Sloss

Published in Columbia, South Carolina, by the
University of South Carolina Press

Manufactured in the United States of America

01 00 99 98 97   5 4 3 2 1

Library of Congress Cataloging-in-Publication Data

Sloss, Henry, 1941–
  The threshold of the new : poems / by Henry Sloss.
    p. cm. — (The James Dickey contemporary poetry series)
  ISBN 1–57003–234–3 (cl). — ISBN 1–57003–235–1 (pb)
  I. Title. II. Series.
PS3569.L685T47 1997
811'.54—dc21   97–21150

"Leaving the Old, both worlds at once they view
That stand upon the Threshold of the New."
—Marvell

For Gigi,
who let me see
what love would make of me

CONTENTS

A NOTE ON HENRY SLOSS

Very few men and women have the energy and the nerve to reinvent their lives. And of these few, only a minor handful have been poets, responsible to such reinvention in terms of . . . in terms, at all. Since Dante, we have learned that the responsibility of renewal is a matter of the soul's society (and solitude), and that the reach of the language is an entirely exorbitant extention. Yet like some others, as I shall indicate, the poet of *The Threshold of the New* has had the energy, and the poems themselves demonstrate, in all the *sprezzatura* of their adept designs, that he has still, Lord knows, the nerve: his is the new life determined upon by slicing himself away from the old, and his are the poems which record the daily blessings of that severance duly perceived, indefatigably acknowledged, indelibly rendered! The strangeness—strange *to us,* of course; to him nothing is strange except what is not so—inheres in the decor, not the decorum. Henry Sloss made his New Life out of the Old World, found his virgin timbers among old stones, the Mediterranean matrix, residing in Italy, roving about Greece as an outsider among those most intensely at home, a borderer in lands most traditionally central.

There have been other Henrys who have done as much, or as well—Henry James, who found the Italian simplicities quite unimaginably blank:

The charm was, as always in Italy, in the tone and the air and the happy hazard of things, which made any positive pretension or claimed importance a comparatively trifling question; we stayed no long time, and "went to see" nothing; yet we communicated to intensity, we lay at our ease

ix

in the bosom of the past, we practiced intimacy, in short, an intimacy so much greater than the mere accidental and ostensible: the difficulty for the right and grateful expression of which makes the old, the familiar tax on the luxury of loving Italy . . .

and Henry Miller, who discovered in the Greek stones a kind of answer to the questions he had not even known how to ask:

The Greek earth opens before me like the Book of Revelations. I never knew that the earth contains so much; I had walked blindfolded, with faltering hesitant steps . . . The light of Greece opened my eyes, penetrated my pores, expanded my whole being. I came home to the world, having found the true center and the real meaning of revolution.

But theirs is not the lineage I would direct a genealogizing reader to trace in "placing" this new poet whose new threshold abuts so familiarly upon the landscapes of *Italian Hours* and *The Colossus of Maroussi.*

Let me suggest, rather, that Henry Sloss belongs in a trajectory which swings back (or forward: in poetry such directions are reversible, the world is round) from James Merrill (to whom he dedicates, in fact, the very poem in which he actually says:

The poem proceeds through likenesses, absurd
Though it may seem to think of chance as meant,
Until a world that would not have occurred

To us becomes both real and heaven sent.)

to Ezra Pound, who also turns up in these poems so knowingly, so necessarily, as the epigraphic master of "A Foreign Medium," that ounce of prevention against a Poundian cure. It is a bearing, as the heraldists say, of the divided life, in Pound as in Merrill dependent upon a perspective of Exile and Return. And I believe the perspective is given its true dimension, its stereography one might say, by eliciting the third and grandest figure in this poet's native strain [*sic*], that progenitor of all Happy Exiles in modernity, Lord Byron. The various (often simultaneous) attitudes of humility, heroism, and haughtiness surface most impressively in Henry Sloss, though what was haughty in the Lord is merely (merely!) and impudently happy in the loner: out of such loneliness, Apollo's arms are wrought, are wielded, are won!

Richard Howard

ACKNOWLEDGMENTS

These poems have been previously published as follows:

Amaranth
      "Penelope's Travels"
Hellas
      "Death by Beauty"
Poetry
      "The Cat Songs"
      "The Parthenon"
      "The Wedding at Vernazzano"
The Paris Review
      "Between Lives"
Tucumcari Literary Review
      "Civic Pride"
Western Humanities Review
      "An Old World Setting"
      "Olive Culture"

PART I

PENELOPE'S TRAVELS

When the time came to go,
I left myself behind:
   That way you know
Someone is keeping you in mind.

   The trip has gone to hell.
Off on my own for once
   But not well,
I have thought about myself for months.

She combs through seas and Cyclades,
   Light-fingered at her loom;
He paces memory's
   Narrowing room.

BETWEEN LIVES

If you were fired and were free to go
From Appalachia to
The Apennines, would you
Think twice before you flew,
With wife and child in tow,
To the Old World and to a new
Life at Lake Trasimeno?

As his cohort brushes up
on customs, readies baby, passport, map,
terra firma rushes up,

Jolts a soldier from his nap—
the hero of lost battles and failed wiles—
lands him in the Old World's lap

Roughly, say, a million miles
from where, like spring's first pitch, he was thrown out
to the crowd's contagious smiles.

Partisans appear to sprout
from Rome's mobbed airport's tangle and to sweep
three tired troopers from the rout

Through the sunset to a steep
starlit road, winding up somewhere above
scenes unseen except in sleep.

One of them is dreaming of
a world as precious to him as his breath,
lost as causes, job, and love,

When he wakes gasping for air, scared to death.

> How far we go, how little we know
> Of even the world we leave;
> How easy to believe
> The new will be a breeze,
> Or at worst a three-day blow,
> Above the gray-barked olive trees
> And ash-white Trasimeno.

After a half hour of steam,
the hand at his throat, foot pressed to his chest
seemed to ease and he could dream

Things had worked out for the best;
but when the windows showed the world immersed
still in darkness, he confessed

Things had worked out for the worst.
History was the nightmare he had read
it was; politics were cursed;

Even Revolution bred
more fat cats by transmogrifying mice,
who had better have been dead,

Into felines, vice by vice,
felonious appetite for power by lust . . .
—cheese he tasted once or twice.

Whether the closed house's must
and dust, or sunset's rust, choked him, a yawn
cleared the way for him to just

Surrender to suggestions of a dawn.

> Although this took place years ago,
> September of 72,
> That ageing ingenu,
> At ripe old thirty-one,
> Knew everything I know
> Except that his life had just begun
> At gray-green Trasimeno.

Soon as he had left the chill
of the box-like cottage, copses of pine
drew his eye far down the hill.

"Cloudy mass without outline,"
he began, "if you are Lake Trasimene,
will you favor our design?

"Can a simple change of scene,
a year's lease on a house in paradise,
matter? What does pretty mean?

"Justice has been my device
for so long, how can olives, tree by tree
brought to light by the precise

"Fingering of dawn, touch me?
What has a world of beauty to do with
war, racism, poverty?

"Or is equity a myth?
Candor and independence variegation
for self-interest's monolith?"

The wilderness is no place for vacation.

        What becomes of the injured ego
        Without the aid of others,
        When bathing one another's
        Wounds had seemed so ideal?
        Can poetry bestow
        What never was—the power to heal
        On milky Trasimeno?

Gentle Reader, if you are
there at all, can you see me as I am
figured in these lines, so far

Gone on innocence, a lamb
thrown to the lions could not feel less guilt?
Notwithstanding the enjamb-

Ment of a late (sticky) gilt-
edged love interest's blurring the period,
righteousness remained unspilt.

Actually I felt an odd
comfort in culpability, saw even
there the even hand of god.

Some impurity would leaven
the hell I would describe in poetry,
once we settled into heaven.

Other people seem to see
the comic features of our self-conception
much more easily than we,

For whom self-knowledge is of self-deception.

> Again at ripe old fifty or so,
> Where ripeness shows as gray,
> An ageless naïveté
> Makes me feel like a dope.
> Do you, do others go
> Through lives as free of muddying hope
> As transparent Trasimeno?

Tasteless as this self-abuse
may seem, what would self be without its spice?
Piquancy is my excuse

For browbeating someone twice
as well-meaning as I could ever be
again; someone just as nice

To friend as to enemy;
a man whose faults were generous in kind
as mine are in quantity.

Out of it, where "it" is mind,
he thinks his suffering in a good cause should
be rewarded. Is he blind,

Or am I? I know I would
not tell him everything I know today,
even if somehow I could.

He will learn along the way
the wages of his virtue, for the cost
comes to more than I dare say

To anyone so proud as he and lost.

DEATH BY BEAUTY

Almost from the first hours in Italy
my breathing failed me literally.

Wheezing (from asthma, not then diagnosed)
pursued me like an unlaid ghost.

Less on day-trips, more at night in our stale
rental, I heard its fusty tale.

For stifling incubi of cob-webbed, glue-
filling lungs woke me and were true.

But because I was uninitiated
in bronchial lore, I thought the overstated

Beauty of Umbria would be my death:
from the first hours it took my breath.

I mean the earth and sky, the terraced hills,
light turning olive leaves to quills;

The well-groomed fields, combed through by the same hands
balancing fruit in market stands;

The cornucopia of children poured
from an old master's drawing board.

I wondered, sighing at sight after sight,
if I would die of them that night.

ON TOP OF THE WORLD

As high up in Assisi as it goes,
one comes to get an eyeful—and a nose.

Of beauty first: from near to far the scene
intrigues its witness. What does beauty mean?

Tiled roofs, like eyelids closed at the first hints
of sunset, color with its deepening tints;

Dusk fills the valley, makes the Tiber seem
alluring as a willow-lined trout stream;

Blood-reddening the sky the sun goes down
behind what was a fierce Etruscan town.

Perugia that would be, famed now (who misses
the past?) for fashion and dark chocolate "kisses."

— Of urine second: for at last its reek
Takes over as the sight-seer's eyes grow weak.

His predecessors' pungent message reads
Beauty means nothing to unpretty needs.

The first stars shine in windows far below;
down is the one direction left to go.

PROSPECTS FROM GUBBIO

I

We came here first with our best friends in Europe,
People we hardly knew, but friends indeed
For guiding us from Customs, around Rome,
And through the dog-days' heat to Umbria:

A Swiss newspaperman, his wife, their child,
An unexplained young German intern, sweet
On Sibil (she indulged him, shared her cones
With him as with her unweaned two-year-old).

Art is her husband's passion, art not found
Hung in museums, so he plans vacations
Around pursuing beauty even unto
Dank chapels in deconsecrated churches.

We went wherever their ménage was going,
Toward an old fresco or new infidelity;
What better introduction to a world
Elusive as its tangled tongues?

Unless it was the future figured in
A bouquet offered, bought in the dark street
We groped down toward our favorite trattoria:
Petalless stems sprinkled with strong perfume.

II

In the succeeding weeks we found ourselves
Alone with incommunicable sights
(There is no telling Rome, Siena, Venice),
Insights from guidebooks we had time to read,

Long lessons in the mother tongue of silence:
The summer people we had just met left;
Friends did not write; we did not understand
Much of what we were hearing locally.

Found ourselves pregnant with our plans for staying
In the Old World—why go back to the known,
When there is everything to learn right here?—
And with a sibling for our two-year-old;

Found ourselves going back to Gubbio,
Climbing to its piazza's paradigm
Of the hill town sublime, then hurrying
From the cold to our favorite trattoria.

Itself so cold we saw our breaths embodied
Over lunch, drank wine from a warmed carafe,
And wondered about ghostly friends,
As numerous once as chairs at empty tables.

CIVIC PRIDE

The tourist trade in Tuoro
Looks slack again this year,
Because as God the Fodor knows
There's nothing here.

A nondescript piazza,
Overlooking the lake,
Stares inward at an empty fountain—
For pity's sake!

Yet local people think
Themselves in luck
To live where passersby believe
Them stuck.

For Tuscany beyond the hills
We really do not care;
Self-satisfaction comes from being
Without compare.

No wonder I am happy
Where no one thinks to ask
Why I am always smiling
Or what smiles mask:

A vision of busloads
Who some day come to see
The larger-than-life-sized equestrian
Likeness of me.

AEROGRAM FROM UMBRIA

Each hill town wears a raiment
of different colored light:
Perugia's red, Assisi's rose,
Gubbio's white.

The fields between, in green
mottled with poppy stain,
mark the inhuman union of
beauty and pain.

The postcards, poorly made,
cannot do justice to
the sights I see as loneliness
tightens its screw.

Distance dissolves in air
so clear I realize
our having been so close made me
believe my eyes.

Opaque Lake Trasimene,
gray olive and white ox
pronounce the unseen in the seen
orthodox.

I am so happy here
I keep holding my breath,
so miserable I pass the time
planning your death.

Am I out of my mind
from being out of your sight?
Forgive my putting it this way:
you better write.

LOVE LETTER

Have you been to Gubbio?
Have you been to Todi?
I'm asking as though you were here
And you would hear.

I haven't heard from you at all:
Have you forgotten me?
Dropped me as an emotional
Luxury?

If you were in Gubbio,
If you were in Todi,
We could talk, maybe even smile,
About exile.

When local people speak to me,
I wonder what is said;
I know what it is like to be
As good as dead.

Seeing me in Gubbio,
Seeing me in Todi,
You'd think the scene itself would buffer
What one could suffer.

But beauty is a quill, a shiv,
Unless you're on vacation;
It sticks you with the life you live
In isolation.

Walking around Gubbio
Or around Todi,
Because you're all I have in mind,
Guess what I find?

Your features, opening at my feet
Against the fan-work stone;
Closing the serpentining street:
Leave me alone!

You are in Gubbio
And Todi,
Blinding me to all I see
But enmity.

BOCCA DI LEONE

*The name of anyone suspected of being a
danger to the State could be dropped into
the mouth of a bronze lion's head.*

Too thrilling sunlight's depth
charge plunges through the sea;
if I were not so sunk
it might move me.

All the concussion hurls—
beam, rigging, compass, bunk—
sails until the shock's finished,
then settles, changed, diminished.

A dark cloud's passage ends
in screwing's raucous curls;
I'm ok without friends,
better off without breath.

Relief maps ridge the sand;
I like it being dead;
let someone else's hand
feel for the lion's head.

Venice, 1973

THE CAT SONGS

I. Milk to Milk

Sweet and sour, she laps all,
from a bone-white china saucer:
hers the power, ours the hour.

Diamonds keen as fright and towering,
they devour as they lour;
she ignores nor high nor fallen.

Froward, coward, each she scours,
skims each son withal, each daughter:
all is pour to her pur-night.

Milk our foster, milk our birth-right,
watering down her maw, we shower.

II. Catechism

She is given, is the way,
hers the passage of all sorrow;
all who live are wholly shriven.

Hell is harrowed, here our voyage—
something vivid to ship in;
far to leeward day we're driven.

Once we quicken, once we stiffen,
gone today is gone tomorrow:
pipe no Captain or last Mast.

Pray no salvage, rig no heaven,
running narrows into clay.

III. Splitting Hairs

Air to shivers, the sun breaks;
day declines to definition;
light our livery, dark delivery.

From decision comes design,
fit is jittery till it's hers;
Fashion's predicate is scissors.

Here a snippet, there a sliver,
sheared appears divine, then quivers:
schism is the maker's mate.

Bared we wait her spare precision,
to a whisker close her line.

IV. Alba

Hold their peace, the unarmed throng,
singled out of breath to innocence:
quiet keeps for soundless sleepers.

Mourning songs belong to vigilants,
furtive reveilles no one heeds:
parting company's left us restless

Here: police and uneasy treaties,
new bereft through other sund'rings,
crises' sibyllance and bruit dawn.

—Lonely matins clench with death, O
caterwauled song: Let freedom cease!

V. Epitaph: For a Suicide

Thought snows: ought I as you do,
reason blizzards out of dying,
seize the cold before I'm frozen?

Thinking too is death-defying,
where what blows is your *what for?:*
ours the coals death cats about.

Smoldering at your cold shoulder,
burning for the ice without you,
unto you true I flame, "no."

Others' winds warm doubt to thawing,
love is lying still as dew.

A FOREIGN MEDIUM

"How is it far if you think of it?"

The Pisan Cantos

I. Tourists

A painter's rag dropped in a hospital corridor

Stationed by the path to the brilliant edifice,
Trecento gold below and blue above,
Gypsies in gypsy-motley litter the approach
To the Basilica of Saint Francis, begging

They are themselves
As little interested in Europe's history as we
In adding them to our itinerary

They have come as we have come for us

When I wondered where we were
Rex seemed testy but that's Rex
I was thinking
                 when he said
Two-thirds through the Travellers Cheques
I couldn't believe it

Can you believe the geraniums
                 the pink stone
                         Assisi's

23

Staggering
Jamaica's got the beaches, got the rum

Others know what they are doing
They walk by without letting the gypsies see them
See them
        Do you think they're happy?

Gypsies are said to be happier than we
                richer than we
Who are better off

I mean the people here, appearing between thrown
Back shutters to water geraniums

Assisi's a bore
Except in retrospect or in anticipation
      I couldn't wait to get to Rome
      but all I thought about was home
          watering a chore
The gypsies an impediment to self
   aggrandizement's grand tour

I sometimes lose myself in watering
             my pillow

I thought you said this would be fun
Europe's not for everyone

              Franchi, Signori
What do they want
        How much are you supposed to give them

Said what she wouldn't give
For a taste of the Caribbean, a mess of
         potage *Marchi*

What's the point
                  of all these Churches
It's what they have here
        what's on the menu *Dollari*

I would be happy here except for the gypsies
That baby's filthy
                  those girls beautiful
Rex says they do it deliberately
                        Hold on
            to your purses
Shouldn't we give them something *Pietà*
            to satisfy our consciences
I haven't got anything small enough

Some offerings they disdain, pocketing them anyway
How much to have you change
Your arrogance for poverty of spirit *Grazie*

We know even less of you than we know
Of Giotto blue and Cimabue gold
In the great double Church of San Francesco
But we can get around if not over you
                  Al'inferno, Signori

II. A Visitor

        Pale Father—
An English Franciscan ferries the strangers
Down the steep outside stairs, shows you
Through a double portal into the dark hold of the lower church

Banked candles, choirs of prayer for the dead, pool light,
But the arterial maze of the chapels and passageways dampens it
                  Theirs is not enough
Lire-lit lamps illumine the frescoed walls and vaults;

25

The Padre explains in part and then passes on
                              —O take me on!

"St Francis wished his grave to lie
With outlaws' here on what was called Hell Hill,
But for the love he bore his friend
Brother Elias denied him his will.

"He spirited the corpse away
To St George's, now St Clare's, as Hell is Paradise;
Pope Gregory canonized
in St Sebastian's chapel to the left

"The relics, his vestments
Hang; parallel lives retouched by others;
Lombard Gothic Sienese scenes;
Giotto dressed as Mary Magdalene

"The Virgin and the Papal Bull
Mutilation general
Martinis"

                    An American woman once asked me
                              if there were any relation

                 I remember stars like unextinguished cinders
                              burning out up a black flue

          The church like a runaway car
in an old-fashioned film
                    is still,
careering disasters projected before it
Over the church the sky veers

                    and one February fall of snow

outside the Merton Chapel
trailing its petticoats down the path to the left and then
lifting before my eyes
a sheer crinoline

I told her there was no relation
between the cocktail and the Sienese's
slit-eyed sirens
posed as saints
None I knew or cared to know, although
Each is of a world intoxicating to its celebrants
There is no relation but negation

Always they have questions of me
Where are you from, when will you return
do I miss my tea
I shall stay where I am
La Beatrice mia is a man

some days I am not myself

Negation of negation
Dissimulated simulation
like the filming in an old-fashioned film
Mock-illusion stills illusion
But is illusion still, ungodly

some days I feel possessed

I understand the stigmata and the sun
The love of Francis for
His Works
But the art of man is blasphemous,
Desecration in the church

Look at the commotion in the kitchen
Distracting from The Last Supper
                              the monkey
Strutting above The Flagellation:
What is art but negation

                    as though some Ugolino out of his depth

I have heard the scholars arguing here
Heard them curse and worse
                    at the impiety

Of obscuring Lorenzetti's Crucifixion
With an altar

                    were consuming me

And they don't know! change their minds
As the seasons swing above the church
                    They don't know! but as things go
This one can decide
    Facts the next one will deride

They only agree in their capacities
    They set their lines of debate
Among the ignorant
                    and come to negate
        gnawing self-hate

                    They know nothing! students of the smear
                    left and renewed by study
                        they study themselves in despair
                        the wryest expounds the wry
                            authors of their own authority
                                spitting into the wind

28

Negation and dissimulation are
all that remain to
arrogating brains astray in
lesions' fields

Dominating the figure to the right
With a set piece of no mean
Skill and in its day virtuosity,
Cimabue's Madonna and Angels is also the site
Of a brown figure, whose mole mien
Belongs to Francis, it may be

Who else could it possibly be
Such ugliness is its warranty

The truly human is unsightly, poor
Showing at every pore
in every trace
The genius of the race for vanity
All art else is a lie
a disfiguring of man's poverty

And need of grace
as vicious in dissimulation
As the self-satisfaction in a gypsy's face
simulating effacement

Knowledge is knowledge of the smear
of sin, conviction of ignorance
abasement before the birds
and the swirling everchangingeverstatic sky

the rest is lies
cinders in God's eye

I shall never be reconciled to the visible church
forgive its eruption against the sky
or its simulated Paradise
where demons enter

Damn you, all who come to prey

III. Space

Thrust out! beyond its gravity
The past coalesces beneath your eyes . . .

As a window pane
may be
in the course
of a stone's trajectory
cause and coordinate of irregular apogee
(& broken)
deceleration following
I had a dream

My torso seen from just ahead
And just above, *I* as I am
To my own unreflecting eyes,
I have come back to Assisi

I had thought to seek the future
Of the poem by going back
To the place where it had begun,
The site which became its setting

The full-length features of desire
Flickered in the short subject:
To "go back" is to go back to
The past, as it comes back to you

So *"Mom" is here, The Campers' "Mom"*
("Pop" was not; my father is "Dad"),
And *two fraternity brothers*
Sitting at dining hall tables

I recall the two as a team:
A short dark "Stan" and his round blond
Ollie of a pal, recast as
The stars in this "old-fashioned film"

The rectangle at which I write
Is as rectangular as where
I ate at Camp and at the Frat:
The tables are the tables' shape

The wit is in the editing:
The splicing does not distinguish
Mother from Mother, past from past,
Or Franciscans from frat brothers
                         Is there reason to?

      The leading man without a face
The camera and audio
For this still obscure production
Got his start in San Francisco

The properties imply a meal
And *I am prompted to perform*
Some propitiatory *burlesque,*
For *I have changed* but *they have not*

As though the movies of your lives
Stuck at a particular frame,
And I was the projectionist,
I thought to move you with my art

31

I wash my hands, though they are clean,
To present them ("Good boy for Mom"),
But as *I hold them out, palms up,*
I see they are shaking badly

I dreamt that I could use its props
To animate the stage-struck past,
But who not if the dreamer knows
You only get away with change

Across indeterminate space,
*I make a*nother *pitch to them:*
"What are you guys still doing here?"

Behind me (the back of my mind?)
A stock of extras laughs at what
I do not think is laughable;
The audience is a ringer

But *the hit line makes me a hit,*
For *the two brothers smile at me;*
I shrug off the success to turn
From them and mask *my bafflement*
        Could *I* have known the joke was on me?

Because *they are all behind me*!
My limelight is their gaiety;
Then *a* straight man's *joke is a flop,*
For *this is* mine, *my company*

I solo at a bare table;
I wait without object and *stare,*
Thinking *I will not be able*
To eat whatever is brought there
        (Nothing was)

                    The altered light is intercepted
                         by the screen
             We say, "The movie's *there*"

Between full waking and the dream,
The space in which the dream is known
To be a dream, unreal, art,
But before coming to is coming back

I saw the features of a friend
Whom I recalled by his last name.
        Sometimes you see things that you know
Are not there; some you call *your* memories.

Stationed by the path to
                         the Frat,
A rushee, *me,* watched another,
A "legacy," come up the path
Bent to like
            Cimabue's Madonna.

I think I recognize him but
Decide not to say anything—
It is important to be cool—
But *my* hot mouth says, "Hi, Mickey!"

His gaze was so aggressively
Blank that the party scarcely paused
To frown and swept into the Church:
"Mickey" had grown up into "Mike."

He is the only one I knew
At both camp and fraternity;
The memory provides a link
Between the two, identifies
                    me with the gypsies.

33

I had thought my interest other.
Is all that I find
                fetching
                        me?

. . . moving away it takes on hue and size,
But the past is not where you would have it be.

IV. Mind Game

22 Feb/Festa di Santa Margherita da Cortona
Played pinball in Cortona
Went back to Assisi, but the gypsies
        were gone as
The Renaissance, gone
                as The Revolution, bought
A round-trip ticket to Rome

The wind makes of this corny *casa all'Italiana*
In Umbria a beached hull

                ma mi domando
Should you loose your hold when the flood turns,
                sink in the thick sea
Or hang on and be battered to bits by the surf

Say you begin again with whatever of worth
                        is left over
To see how foreign parts will weather it
        Some foreign particles become pearls
                but in particulars
                        nature is not to be appealed to

Would you say nature knows
                        what it is doing?

34

Cross examination of the trees reveals
                                   the groundlessness
                    séi matto, séi
Of the interrogator's case, but ice
                         glazing the flowering almonds
Makes it appear that nature errs

Do you recall, after we had made land,
                 anyone's suggesting we burn the ship?

                              Cortona

          Assisi

     Renaissance

               Rome

If history is natural, civilization born
                              to die
Whatever arises will decline &
                         Say
You come away, arrival is delayed
                         fall

If associations are unfree, your thinking may be
                 said to be done for you

                    Say
     you come to drink at the stone stoup of

                         absence
          & find yourself
                    arraigned by the proverb of absence
                    living its corny text, dogged

By the experience of others, by the past
How can you escape the text you illustrate?

                                    Touching down
Begins with a critical reading:
            the text is always absence
                                    the lack of what
Present would make the text unnecessary
                        fond

Went back to Assisi

                    gone

This is the very Chapel of St. Martin
As though in imitation of a line of Shelley's
                    Simone Martini
Or someone very like Simone Martini
                                    arranged the stained glass
                        arraigned the white radiance so

When the sun is unclouded
                            colored light
            discolors
                    gli affreschi di chi?
Buon dì, EP
        or someone very like Simone Martini

And you, did you mistake these Indians
            who got so much else right?

Time in course will favor you
                        draw the polemics from your lines
                                    like salt from sea water
                        forget the difference between

36

                    Pilgrim & Ghibelline, Guelf & Puritan
Time blurs school & party, tribe & sect

Like an ill wind in February
                  forgetfulness is natural

Before love fails into its opposite
                it turns to hate
Holding to its power to draw all things about it
Like a great coat in foul weather
                drawn up about the neck
But it twists the head at last

                    Sail on, Intemperate Pilot
For whose sake who would not
                have had the stars fixed

                the gypsies
      gone
          gone
        The Revolution

You leave the Brethren before you take off
The sea flew against the vessel and broke
                  into our stores
We shored up whatever of worth
            is left over
With memory, making it difficult to land

After coming ashore
Things take their colors from distrained eyes
            First we scrawl Croatan
Have our Thanksgivings
          in despite

Start at the name of Isabel

She sat in the lower church, her face in her hands
We were to enter here and walk through the dark,
The lives of Christ and Francis flanking our passage,
Then rise to the upper church, brilliant with light

Side chapels cut into the scheme below
Strain the sunlight through particles of colored glass
Obscure the symbolism with illumination,
Create out of the hell of life an Inferno

She might have been posing for a portrait,
                    Figure of a Girl in Grief

            gone
The Renaissance, gone

                Rome

Can the case change
            with a change in venue?
                        Or do all
Roads lead to the Rome of unconscious character
                        fixed associations, maddening
Remakes of the same scene?

Walking through the Borghese Gardens
            I know myself
                        dogged by my memory of
A young man with a blue bruise under one eye
                        a black dog straining at a choke
            asking me for a smoke
So pleased to understand his Italian
                        I had not seen all of what was wanted

In character, *Narciso senza un pozzo*
    longing led me at the closed Museum
            to look into windows
Made partially opaque by reflection,
                to pace the paths entranced by
            what I missed

Those who are excluded have no history
            except exclusion
In default are granted a kind of timeless interest
            even at odd moments
An odd sagacity for keeping free
Of what refuses them entry

Cast out of an old life, I found my way
            to outcasts

Thought to lose myself in others
                like me not me
            by submitting to the touch of
                a foreign medium
As though by calling it *esilio*
    I would be spared the fact of my exile

Played pinball
                gypsies

  Renaissance
        Revolution
 round-

Today in the Borghese the Museo is open
    I pass by the antique, the weak chin of Tiberius
        thinking

You are not what you can remember,
    but what you cannot forget

                Come to
Bernini's Daphne, at longing's touch
          turning in grief
               to another nature,
                        rapt
As her stone fingers become leaves
I feel myself change

Huddled around their got-up history
Early on they cracked
               the record of the Paris Commune
The Pilgrims beat their winters out Odd
        given what would follow
            no one suggested burning the ship

A casa in the hills of Umbria
    as in the untoward medium of art
It is so cold, only desire
To realize your loneliness warms
               you

There is no
        other cold
There is no end but an end to ardor
flipflipflipfliptilt

40

PART II

CALYPSO'S ISLAND

Months become years. Obsessions burn
Themselves out,
Disappear in pride's doubtful
Victories over yearning.

What's more, Penelope is here
Drinking in the sun,
If that's she. I don't wonder
At changes in appearance.

Home, the magnetic monolith
Steered by, has come
Down to the compass
Of this Ithaca.

OLIVE CULTURE

Today we walked the hills behind the house
Through terraces of olives—some still worked,
Others less accessible abandoned
To broom and scrub oak and the olive grown,
Lacking cultivation, in on itself.
(Traces of fire that swept the hilltops bare
As a hearth still show through here and there).
So many trees, so many terraces
Of trees appear to have been left without
Once looking back, we were surprised
To find the price for half a stone farmhouse
Figured in terms of its two fields of olives.
Why we came to buy it with the little
We had left is more than I can say.
In part our marriage of ten years required
Some gesture, asked that we spend all we had
To gain this purchase against going home
Empty-handed. That we would learn to think
Of here, of Umbria, as home would follow
And would come easier to our two boys,
Little as they are, little as they know
Of other homes or straitened circumstances.
Our lunch guests won't have thought of us as cramped,
Given such a meal in such a setting;
For even on a wet December day
The round maternal beauty of these hills
Above the lake, above the glow
From dark red wine and heaping plates of pasta,
May be imagined to have fairly shone.

Those of us whose aim was exercise
Set our sights on a rundown farmhouse,
Abandoned but intact, just visible
From where, swayed by so much lunch and from being
So long rained in, we gave ourselves to slogging
Upward.
        The road ran silver, the road ran
Out for the two lovers. We left them gazing
From a turning into winter sunlight,
The almost artificial incandescence
Of a short-lived (a furtive?) holiday.
Who knows why lovers turn in on themselves,
Away from those who need love most, who stare
Like stricken children at its chilling flame?
So only three of us, two grown men shadowed
By a boy (as grown men tend to be),
Assailed the hill, tacked at rose hips and oak,
And steering by the farmhouse navigated
The terrain.
        Grown still more slippery since
The evening rains that followed our long walk,
Our guests' departure and the coming of
The first dark of the night. Grown treacherous
Too for the dog so used to sitting up,
As at the wind's whistling, to chase his tale.

All day a parking lot came back to me,
A sun-washed opening between old haunts
(An opening is all a poet wants):
A smoky pool hall and a bright bookshop.
The first place featured sharks at play
(Do poets too need blood to find their way?);
Trying to be polite by keeping something
Between us as the fatherly shopkeeper
Bore down on me, struck as he seemed to be

And caromed back and forth between
Certain proprieties and sure desire—
Time's gauntlet run among fine old editions—
Was what was playing at the other place.
(One likes to think oneself desirable,
However little one would be pursued,
Perhaps because, as any child can tell you,
Love is forbidden where it is desired).

The rain lessens and the fire paves its way
In ash, but the wind threatens to raise the roof.

"Everyone complains about the weather,"
My father used to say, "but no one ever
Does anything about it." He still may,
Though not to me. I moved away for good
A dozen years ago and have kept going,
But as the boys grow up I seem to be
Taken back. I have always kept in touch.
Recently the long-distance salesman's line
"As good as new" recalls another standby,
"Salesmen sell themselves."
                                    The doctors say
The heart is better for its being opened.

The boy has never seen his father cry
Although tears were the amniotic fluid
In which I grew a proper crocodile.
We ate our family dinners on the Nile,
When we could eat. Breaching a mother's faith
In good manners, the good they would do us,
Would issue in Homeric showstoppers:
First she would be "a Trojan," then Achilles.
At last she left the table and the scene
Was played out in the wings: closed doors opened

To argument, apology, and tears
Of reconciliation at the flood.
(You learn important lessons at the table:
To chew with your mouth closed, to speak only
When spoken to, and so to withhold love
As to protect yourself from getting hurt).
I was the one who made up to and with
My mother, but who could not make up for
The disappointments of her life. Children
Know they are to blame, but do not know
For what. I knew my father over-matched,
Knew because he loved her he was helpless,
Knew he was listening for the storm to pass.

Now what was raging sighs, two stars appear
To disappear, their high light overcast.
But is it any wonder if I find
Men disappointing, women dangerous
Even to this day? When I was fired
My father said, "You cannot stand success,"
As though I sought to realize myself
By being disappointing in my turn.
Children do not understand success
Or what it means to be provided for,
Though they know what it is to lack protection
From forces they cannot control, like love
And hate and shame, know what it is to hope
That growing up will end their helplessness.
(I do not think my father could have known,
Baffled as he was, abashed by my mother's
Temper and as powerless against it
As a child, that his children understood
Him as providing them with an example
Of how love victimizes anyone).
As the fire dies down the heating stove cools;

The ashes make me wonder if there is,
Has ever been, a bed to lie in
Whose truth is not that any life you make
Must either be consuming or consumed.

When we got to the farmhouse and looked back
The boy was, in a boy's determined way,
Still making his way slowly up the hill.
The boy in me identifies with him.
I wonder how they differ if their fathers
Both express love in helplessness.
My feelings for the boys unman me:
I know a mother's feral passion for
Their physical well-being and a child's
Delight at feeling love reciprocated,
The same child's fear that through some fault of his
The love will end. I seem to have become
My father with my mother's temperament,
And so seem bound to disappoint and bully
The boys until they fly from me in turn,
In order to protect themselves from love.
How can I hope to have their love one day
If I cannot forgive my dying father's
Not being what I needed him to be?
As such the prospects are not promising.

The boy was happy to have come this far,
So near another world at that world's brink;
For if he found the house's vacancy
Scary and understood how empty casements,
Staring blindly out, let the weather in,
Expose the house's insides to unfeeling
Elements, his eye was drawn as well
To lines of quicksilver the rain had sown
In furrows far below. Does silver grow?

He watched and listened while the other two,
Habitues of how, grown up, you do,
Smoked a Kool apiece and dreamed aloud
Of building in the swale below the house.
The road could be improved, the house's stone
Reused, and the abandoned land
Redeemed by being plowed again, reworked;
We talked too of rebuilding terraces
Where the stones, set in place time out of mind,
With time become dislodged.
                            A cultivation
That the hills did not wholly disbelieve.
Coming down we came across the two lovers
Not far from where they left us far behind.

Looking out from the porch of the stone house
At the surrounding circle of dark hills,
Knowing myself surrounded by dark circles
Of memory (from which these emissaries
Appear to represent the deathless past,
A flickering fire that, though it may die down,
Cannot go out), I guess my place must be
Here in the last light of another day
Between the hemispheres of two dark worlds.

The olive matures slowly and at thirty
Is just beginning its productive life,
Except where fire or demographic factors
Result in giving up its cultivation.
Then green shoots finger up and out to close
It in their fist, as though the tree's vitality
Worked against it, turned it in on itself,
Made it unrecognizable as such.
(I too have grown half-wild in these hills, felt
Abandoned and uncultivated, burned

By my experience, and am unsure
What has become of me). You would not know
The green knot for olive, imagine opening
Its heart would bring the tree to bear again
The precious burden of its bitter fruit.
Here the danger is development,
The land cleared, plots laid out, foundations sunk,
Burning in minds more furious than fire.

Lake Trasimene, 1975

LESSON FROM A BESTIARY

Early for the early train to Rome,
I paced a platform in the Tuscan sticks
Wondering what you have in mind for me,
How literary lions do their tricks.

A handsome monkey calls your room, says *Wait*
Sleepily—no wonder he's a clerk:
You ought to wake up early to your fate
When getting nowhere with your work.

After an hour the monkey looks amused;
I'll walk to the Castel Sant'Angelo;
Initiates are easily confused
With others, when the going gets so slow.

At last the hotel's ancient *ascensore,*
A rattling, halting tight-fitting cage you
Crowd into, takes us up to—*Oh, Signore!*—
The roof-top garden's panoramic view

Of the eternal city's seven hills,
Bright as the promise in the warm spring sun.
A finger run along my forearm chills
Me to the bone. The lesson has begun.

At lunch in the Piazza I'll tell jokes,
Wolf down my roast *abbacchio,* swill white wine;
Bird-like you pick at "perfect" artichokes.
Sip mineral water, keep your eye from mine.

Shadows gathered as a kind of Mayan
Grimace became your parting grin's last note:
The lamb who fails to lie down with the lion
Only succeeds in cutting its own throat.

THE DARLING & THE LOVE

If three's a crowd, this first night's overflowed:
One barkeep and two couples at their table
Welcomed me to Athens. Wrapped in fable,
The owner soon appeared but as soon showed

Himself a different man, apologized,
And went out in a heavy overcoat.
My guide was calm. For him change underwrote
The changeless *Darling. He* was not surprised.

From the beginning I was unbelieving
And took his stories for extravaganzas,
Mid-winter's repertoire of songs and stanzas
Rehearsed for a newcomer's stock deceiving.

My newfound friend (lost long ago) nursed beers,
While Dr. Ouzo's tonic beckoned me.
A Greek, I guess she's Greek, says *"Sprechen sie . . . ?"*
(The table's two men vanish like the years),

Goes off to turn the jukebox to Too Loud,
Dances her ouzo-milky-white clad way
Back to her cousin (as we learn), a fay
In frilly black. The two soon swell our crowd.

But they frown on our drinking all alone.
We buy them costly sodas, drunk like shots.
The barman juggles bills, all THOU SHALT NOTS
So much short change to our lax chaperon.

I hasten to acknowledge nothing
Happened. But nothing often does
For poetry what something does
For love. Love lifts her black-frilled dress
From knee to chin, revealing everything
To my guide. Poetry's white dress,
Concealing something, stays in place,
And puts her darling in his place,
Where nothing might mean anything.

A thousand nights of searching for two girls,
Unattached and "nymphomaniac"
Sent sheer black thrills through desperate adolescents
A way of life or two ago.
I can't recall the places where our fake
ID's and fixed ideas of how to look
Grown up drew smiles from unrelenting bouncers,
But I remember nothing happening.
All we did was drive around and around.
When it gets late we get so intimate
With others, shadows we imagine lovers,
As to shout at them or at the dark.
Our stories in the schoolyard the next day
Put nothing in imagination's way.

Hoping to shed our innocence like clothes
We drove one Sunday morning to the pros.
Finding the place still closed, we go next door
To bowl—strike after strike! What more
Could I want? Too late to retreat
I stand here looking at her feet,
Feeling the cold.
                          She asks, "How old . . .?"
                                           I froze.

But did not worry as I ran,
Knew nothing was where stories all began.

                    Half way down
Another ouzo acted up.
My exit line, "This really is strong stuff!"
Draws catcalls from the players prompting me
To redeem years of nothing happening.
The Darling's dim interior steps back
A step and whirls
Out of indifferent arms
For I am in Aegean wind and dancing,
Beneath the lemon trees and orange trees,
To nothing's freezing piper who will pay
For waltzing me away.

I wonder in another winter's chill
How to return and if I ever will.

Calm told Unbelief, "*Love*'s across the street,"
Owned too by the apologetic boss;
When I looked in, though, I was at a loss
To see beyond its being empty.

THE PARTHENON

Below the monastery the mundane
Enchantment of an elegant light lunch,
Reflected in a silver chocolate bowl,
Swallows the other-worldly whole.

Gone now a world of poverty and olives,
Where loneliness can hit you like a low blow;
No wonder the despicable beau monde
Charms an ex-revolutionary hobo.

He minds his manners, quickens to the wit
Flashing, like sunlight through the scattered cloud
And frosted glass, around the candlelit
Foyer, where politics is disallowed.

Next, the initiate attempts a flight
Of treacherous steps and finds himself above,
Attending to a priest of art and love
In a bay windowful of Greek sunlight.

He hears the other, polished as enamel,
Array himself in unrevealing shifts;
And shaggy, heavy-lidded as a camel,
Takes a caliph's interest in such gifts.

A maid of Athens calls upstairs, *Addio.*
The bon-bon mots melt. Spirits slowly slope
Downward and the talk wanders in and out
Of silence, in and out of hope.

Returned then to the city-riddled plain,
He gazes off to where old pillars tell
Stories of heights closed now to Anyman,
Whose consolation must be unbelief.

Athens, 1976

AFTER THE PICNIC

Stealing the sunset's thunder, storm cloud acts
First like a blotter, then seeps up the west
Like ink, forming a sort of Rorschach test
No more to be glanced from than cataracts.

At noon too there were threats. When raindrops come
To blister Polaroids, a rocky brow
With bangs of flowering iceplant shields us from
Whatever Greek spring weather's up to now.

Those clouds blow over and our wary band
Takes heart from having, on its next excursion,
Everything under the sun: wine-dark sand,
A dog's tick drawn out (clock-stopping immersion),

Our three-year-old in over his head
The swelling sea, unnoticed though we shout.
Sunstruck a pink Poseidon would be led
To sum up, *This is what it's all about!*

—In darkness deeper than the night's background
The early stars sink. Lightning, as if vexed
By cliché, strikes at pleasure's shallow text;
Illuminates its depths had the child drowned.

Sounion 1976

GREEK ISLE

The streetlamp cast a net into the sea,
   Draped it along the dock;
Drew schooled and unschooled in the dark,
   Beckoned by its beacon.

A man in sandals probed appearance, pried
   At rocks in the bright pool;
Now one moves—on his pole:
   A fish pierced by its trident.

He grins at his achievement like a god,
   Or like a fisherman
Who does not wonder what fish mean,
   Or by what he is prodded.

Then I move, down the quay, a target for
   Night's pointed imagery,
A brilliant harborful of wry
   Reflections on the foreigner.

What am I doing here, out of my depth,
   Playing games with life,
Tagged after by a mirrored skiff
   Tugging at its tether?

Going nowhere. Place puts another face
   On the self-same abyss:
I am still bound fast to a buoy's
   Empty expectations.

Poros, 1976

59

THE WEDDING AT VERNAZZANO

For James Merrill

For him the second language learned so late,
So little, is, as in Mill's postulate
About the Poet, always overheard.

And so he feels delighted and distressed
At what he understands, as though a guest
Came some way uninvited to the word.

Questo è il Corpo . . . Unreproved
He gets to overhear the priest, more moved
Than he can say to others for whom this

Would be the Body of their Lord—not his,
Whose eyes before he thinks to stop them fill.
Said in English the Mass would no more thrill

Him than it does the couple who won't grieve
Grandparents by ignoring the old way,
But, noncommittal Communists, believe

Hardly at all in. *Questo è il Sangue* . . .

The bells he hears next (gone the bride and groom)
Are not like Sanctus subtle, nor quite boom
Like Wedding. As he wakes his ears ring from

The ringing products of the local vine
Taken at their unlabelled word, the wine
Of work and worry, Labor's kingdom come.

The problem is he drank them like solutions.
To what, his thirteenth hour's resolutions
To fast, to slow, should be survive belie:

Is there an easier way to simplify
Life than to (filled to overflowing) burst?
By wine alone he could not kill his thirst.

Some whiskey then? more cake, ice cream, champagne
On top of lunch in endless courses? Nice
Distinctions fail to rouse the sleepy brain

Rising to chimes and, from the belfry, rice.

Santa Lucia's mouth had held the two
Who once their words have made them one seem to
Shrink from all further speech, from being broken

Into the babbling world where tongues can slip:
Hand in glove they wait at the church's lip
For a flash! The photographer has spoken.

Another country: *Forza con il riso!*
Command hailing the least of us with rice.
—This summer's hail ruined two years of grapes;

No wonder anyone who can escapes:
The sky is not a roof, farming a life.
Talk to this modern husband, ask his wife

About the fields their parents worked, the body
Of lore drawn from long suffering and the hocus
(Eureka! possibly from *Hoc est Corpus*)

Pocus of the Word's unearthly focus.

What's in the word? Do you recall the time
We first met, differed over unsublime
Language & Mind? Words I called "a keyboard

Thought plays." But you, Old Hand, were scarcely sold;
Rather than ivory, you would have words gold;
Told me, "Let language guide your thinking." Floored

As I was by my lucky strike (above),
I grant the word leads landward, like a dove;
But think to crow what might be left unsaid,

Mind must be independent to be led.
If poetry's a way to have the last
Word only when the conversation's past,

I'd trade this chit to chat with you once more.
Or play your game, where animals appear
As images of self. Mine was a wild boar!

Overhear me whose must be a deer.

Time lapse. Perhaps because of all "time" masks,
Its passage may reveal what the poem asks
Of me for its deliverance and mine.

Any day now, the earth will have so spun
Itself through classic movements that the sun
In Vernazzano will be seen to shine

As little as it can . . . *Santa Lucia*!
Giorno più corto che ci sia.

Angels preside, not seen but felt as seeing:
Not the self, they bring the self to being

Keen as a swallow's veering for its prey,
The poet's seeing in a word his way.

The poem proceeds through likenesses, absurd
Though it may seem to think of chance as meant,
Until a world that would not have occurred

To us becomes both real and heaven sent.

LOCUS AMOENUS

Lilac in May,
Almond in March,
Plum in April's seam . . .
    "Buon giorno, Enrico,"
"Buon giorno, Simona,"
    Life is but a dream.

How's life, Simona,
    Will you tell the bard?
'Are long the days,
Are short the years:
    Is hard.'

Cara mia, on that note,
    We'll both go to our hoeing
In different fields
With different yields
    While time is gently flowing.

        *

Locus Amoenus, spelled out by the scholar,
Wooed us, as he did, with a chalky pallor.

At twenty, having lived, we hoped the text
Of the past showed the way to what came next:

Scholarship! Its rejection of the world,
Fading as tans, for the eternal word.

Stragglers in the footnotes to Parnassus,
Few of us would climb beyond the passes
We got in Milton. Put off by the fount
We looked for other ways to reach the mount.

I am surprised to recall anything
From that so distant California spring,
Had thought the latin tag to lost notes tendered
As high ambitions are to Caesar rendered.

*

Beneath the rusty orange ruins at Nauplia
The phrase came back
With morning coffees
In the garden of a Greek King's Arms:
While lemon and lilac
Sing to the bees,
A flowering aviary charms
The misosynesthesiac,
Brings the abstract thinker to his knees.

What grounds remained, like those between my teeth,
For thinking passing happiness beneath
Contempt washed free
In water's sweet transparency.

*

On train trips to our 'pleasant place'
In Umbria, I change in Padova.
Smiles wreathe my face.

The man behind the Station's bar
Declares, to no one in particular,

'Everything is here': "*È tutto qua.*"

He means that paradise and hell
Are in this life (no one comes back to tell
Us otherwise). His clientele,

Departed for their trains, may have concurred,
Though none found time to say the word

While paying on the run for tonic bitters.

*

The garden's grizzled olive, lately picked,
Dozes on through the spring's alarm for sage
And spiny salvia-colored artichoke,
Sleeps through wake-up for apple, plum, persimmon.
Weeds yawn among young peas and runner beans.
Slow carrots, long top-knotted onions, sweet
Basil and tough parsley, delicate dill,
Spiked cucumber and bristle-downed zucchini
Queue up to catch the season's fireworks.
Silently, as in etymology,
Collaboration of old elements
Conspires in seedlings toward the *pomodoro.*
Grape cuttings dig in for a second summer,
While almond trees and fig contrive to hold
Their own in fields whose first delight is olive.
Three young pines mark three Christmases. Three cypress
Mark the road and cannot help but be
Our local, classical memento mori.

*

Oh Contadina, at your rabbit hutch,
Three times the girl who married and was doomed,
In birth, in work, in flesh, to be consumed,
Can you say why, when I am here,
Death is the least thing I would think to fear?

It seems like nothing next to lilac's power
To draw me from the dream that dreams enough
Have come true when the world's in flower:
Nothing, dear neighbor, next to the ambition
To see the lilac in a first edition.

What I see now, white with a smart red comb,
Is watching me, entirely at home,
Until I catch its eye. Then it stalks off,
Making a stiff-legged run for a fig tree
Without the leaf as yet to hide me.

This fear, Simona, is it from a joy
So unconditional I think of Joy
And Grief as two blind singles at a dance,
Who, groping in the dark for partners, touch
One or another, seize on us, by chance?

Or does the poet's fond ambition strain
Beyond the flower of the April rain
Because the lilac's sweet success
Inspires in me the same light-headedness
The morning sun streams through in flying dust?

*

Truth is as truth may be
    Calling me
        From lilac ripe
            Enough to eat;
        From almond scoops
            Of pink and white,
                Melting into green;
        From popcorn blooms
            Young plums revive
            To memory.

At new moon rise
    The traveller sighs,
        Truth is as truth may be.

PART III

TO EURYKLEIA

Please don't let's have a scene!
You know I know
How such shocks thrill,
How much they seem to mean.

How often I have had
Little to show
For them I will
Not to our troubles add

(But sadly heroes are
Admired by no
One for their skill
In covering up a scar).

Self-knowledge and ambition
Abandoned grow
Warm to the chill
Of quiet recognition.

AN OLD WORLD SETTING

I. Klaus' Case

South of Florence, north of Rome,
There is a lake named Trasimene;
Italians know it as the scene
Of infamous defeat;
Nearby—too near what Carmen calls "the only
Ugly town in Italy"—
We have our home away from home.

However much that second home
Shifts with the years, drifts from the States:
Inertia, you could call it, makes of us
Latter-day expatriates;
However much we only come
Here now, to my idea of paradise,
For holidays and summer.

Mildew and harsh fumes of disuse
Wait, while I fumble with the key,
To chastise us for months of inattention;
But in their hurry to abuse
Failings of memory,
There's something *they* forget to mention:
Sensation's finally struck the Summit.

A hamlet built above the lake
For foreigners come to forsake

Their cares, the Summit seems to be
Detached as deity;
But in this case the colony confessed
Itself unable to resist
Rumors surrounding an arrest.

A local favorite for his good
Nature, his pleasant air
Of seeming, like his denim, not to shrink
From any creditable excess,
Klaus, it appears, wove his success
From stuff the worse for smuggling's wear.
No one is quite sure what to drink.

—Off to the west where Carmen and
Roger, her dyed-in-the-wool English husband,
Live in classic renovation
(Old beams exposed to chrome's cheap thrills
And Roger's tight-lipped approbation),
Dark lids fall from the brilliant hills.
—That's plenty for one morning.

Especially since the evidence
From hearsay, from the mud,
Points to rains unloosed in a flood
Of biblical duration. Odd
How an abstract isobar
Lassos the spirit. "Come, now" (Carmen);
"Are you a poet or a lightning rod?"

Customs' raid of the hillside house,
Disdaining peacocks by the pool,
Produced two rifles and a volley
Of blurred allusions to "some fool

American": a cat-and-mouse
Exchange of views the valley,
Preoccupied with peppers, overlooks.

Tobacco grows there too and wheat,
Blanching in the summer heat
Like me when, as I drive
Through on some errand, lost in thought,
A remnant of attention's caught
By fields of poppies. I stop, shocked
By beauty, wonder if I am alive.

Customs smelled something fishy somewhere:
Impropriety's aroma
Attached to pricetags on the silverware;
Frau Klaus, as Carmen calls her, smiles
At inquisition, wiles
A wink away—"Is that a crime?"
Then leaves: "I really haven't time. . . ."

Roger's aplomb somewhat askew,
He hurries to condemn
Such zeal in the authorities: "I mean,
I say, as if ten excise men
Were insufficient for the task,
They drove up in an armored van!
Now, knowing Klaus, I ask you."

Enter K.'s "fool American,"
A long-time innocent abroad
("A dipsomanic denizen
Of foreign shores," says Marian);
Ever a model citizen,
He claims the rifles, flawed
Though his admission is by cracked Italian.

Officialdom will use
His readiness as an excuse
To reperuse an earlier case:
His trigger-happy shots at pigs
"Rooting in *my* asparagus"
Concluded with apologies
Profuse as sandwiches from "*my* prosciutto."

—Dawn again. The author's old
Undergraduate affection
For Eighteenth Century writing owed
To fascination with its beauty mark,
Or affectation, the Digression:
It works like whim against the dark
Providence of the plot.

Lately one side of me has been
Burned by too much of a good thing:
Summer is what comes of spring,
As Carmen comes of Marian.
The latter, a shut-in
No one sees, was to be the heroine
Of a love-interest (smuggled in).

Since the American's confession
Translated into Dutch,
Klaus is to have his company
In the courtroom, if not in jail;
Charged with Negligence in re
The weapons found in K.'s Possession,
The former finds Scotch working where words fail.

"There are no jails in Italy,"
Roger insists: "Klaus is in prison."
The difference would be clearer if

One of his friends had seen him. So far, though,
He is allowed only his wife:
A beauty, ninny, and naif,
She keeps him incommunicado.

Prettily Frau Vanity,
If vanity were ever wed,
Speaks up: "Klaus would do anything for me."
Then looks around as for the sure
Applause she counts on from a mirror;
To doubts in others' eyes,
She's too wise not to toss her head.

An almost irresistible
Speed-up precedes the trial, a sign
To me of almost audible
Anxiety; the lawyers say "A fine
And/or suspended . . .

Fireflies here, moonset over Carmen's.
"Carmen, should an artist . . .?" "*Please,*
Save your sermons on Art and Life
For your—where *is* she?—wife."
Carmen in coral blouse and shawl
Adjusts the lamplight to the twilight,
Takes up her spectacles, lays down the law:

"Analysis is a disease.
I would not think of painting olive trees
As they seem, are, or should be;
I paint my trees until the painting
Suits the artist to a T.
Universality
Comes of what deeply pleases me."

"But, Carmen, these are people." "Are we?
The best of us seem characters
At best; at our worst, actors
In dramas even we deplore."
"But is it right to exploit life?"
"Whatever do you think it's for?
Life vanishes unless it turns to story."

     . . . sentence
Are all the State can really hope for."
What's scarier than confidence?

What's this about plea-bargaining?
What's that about devaluing
The mark against the rising price of jeans?
Seen sharing wine and spaghettini,
Was Klaus' Missis holding hands
With someone whom the Press calls "Hans,"
The Customs men "Houdini"?

Rumors, like cat's-paws on Lake Trasimene,
Appear to disappear
Now that the trial day is here;
It comes up clear, then clouds over;
Nervousness comes over the author;
Ok, what *does* the thunder mean?
Should I have tried to intervene?

Carmen eyes me askance.
"If you had never wished them ill
For the poem's good, you'd feel less guilty;
You needn't fret, they're off scot-free
And celebrating up at Marianne's.

I always told my ex-, Henri,
Anticipation's everything!"

II. A Recipe for Marian

Three cypress take the house's place
In the rearview mirror: we're going down
The narrow dirt road over one,—
Sorry!—a second abrupt bump,
Past eyesores losing stucco's face,
To the road leading left to town,
Right to the public dump.

Marian, the friend I mentioned
As being so elusive—Why?
She stands off and attracts (one moment bastioned
By an aristocrat's reserve,
The next a cheeky shopgirl's verve
Peeps out), like a remote
Schloss circled by a dimpled moat.

She will already be regretting
Having asked to borrow
The tagliatelle recipe
I promised her in time for lunch. I'll show
You the sights while we're driving up.
("Haven't you described the setting?"
"*I'm* the setting!" "Come now, caro.")

Those shrouded hills descending
To the lake draw an unclear line
Between two provinces of mind:
Umbria is unpretending
As her saints; Tuscany's divine.
These fields, one mist-tricked day, saw the refined
Legions fall to trumpeting Hannibal.

The story can be found in—Livy?
I used to know, but living
Here dulls those points and point of view
So critical to visitors
As keen as you; your questions do
Remind me of the sights, the tours
We give up as they cease to see us through.

This lunch is more our cup of tea:
Marian has introduced
Her jet-set sister to our conversation's
Circle, sadly reduced
When Klaus and frou-frau flew the coop;
Of Jean we hear her looks speak volumes,
As do Europe's gossip columns.

(The days no one will see or hear
From Klaus eventually become
Weeks of withering summer,
But now we're getting ahead of ourselves.)
Bees hover, browse the heady shelves
Of lavender for scents, not sound:
"Italy is sacred ground!"

"You're going native, Marian;
How is this country different than,
Say, India?" "Or Minnesota!
Vino, Zippo?" "Zip-pee, man.
Are we the only two Americans
Among these foreign also-rans?"
"Do pass the pasta, Marianne."

"It's lovely, but politically
Italy's a satellite
Looking for a sun—wine, please—

And economically a simply frightful . . ."
"Roger, must you preach?" "Italy's
Not what it used to be."
"Neither is the old grey mirror."

"Why must Americans be rude?"
"He means 'mare.'" "'Mayor' does he mean?"
"Zippy, would you call yourself a Leftist?"
"What do I look like, man, a dentist?
Jeannie, let's split this scene."
"No one has ever called Jean "Jeannie.'"
"She lets me, sister, cuz she likes my weenie."

Amid the pandemonium
Succeeding Zippy's jeu d'esprit,
Jean's eyes—like smoldering smaragdine
Embers in a tan mask—find mine:
"Zippy sucks his thumb
All night, unless his mouth and tongue
Find something sweeter or more savory."

Numinous possibilities
Suggest themselves, as numerous as the breasts
Of the Ephesian Artemis.
We cannot all be devotees:
Carmen scorns "effects
Too obvious for artifice,"
When Jean mistook her proffered sketch.

"Wonderful, Carmen. These
Mandalas . . .?" "Are olive trees."
"And Mr. Croffts, *Roger,* do you
Paint too?" Later this afternoon—
It won't be long—you'll hear Jean try to jolly

Roger out of flag-waving folly,
Marian call him a buffoon.

Where were we? Following the twists
And turns of a road winding
Its way, old olive by new vine,
From Carthaginians to Communists;
The Party has restored the city
Cemetery, long in decline,
Thanks to the new prosperity.

Developing the Summit—
Brain-child of some forgotten Zeus—
From land too poor, too sheer for goats or sheep
But not, for tile-roofed villas, steep,
Brought foreign money to a region
Where economic woes are legion,
And change can seldom have been loose.

Here's what Carmen calls the only
Ugly town in Italy;
"Nondescript" would be too mild;
She's always right, but never fair.
There's the Saint. He's not all there.
Helplessness makes him wild-
Eyed; dentures force his beatific smile.

Here's the Poet. Under cover
Of thick glasses and slept-in clothes
(No one knows as "Nando" knows
The perquisites of Fashion),
The visionary, hard-pressed lover
Of an indifferent Laura holds out for
A poetry of pain and passion.

—Ferdinando, how I wish
What I am cooking were a dish
Fit for your rigid regimen;
The recipe for Marian
Is largely an intestine
Affair whose flavorings I've tried
Fresh, but have found more pungent cut and dried.

"Without the English raj
India would never have been free:
By our example we created Gandhi."
("He's pissed." "He looks pissed off to me.")
"Made him in your image, Rog?"
"Young man, Americans have nothing
Of England's gift for governing."

"Your problem, Rog, is you can't dream
When you grow up of being queen!"
"You are a proper fool. Wine, please."
"Father—out in Burma—kept bees;
Whenever Father worked the hives,
A red flag warned the Dean
Across the way: Beware of swarming lives.

"Father thought the old boy's terror
Inspired those lengthy tracts on human error
He became famous for;
Do you remember, Marian?"
"I loved the nights when Father drew,
By hand, his honey in the loo;
Next morning one's sweet dreams came true."

"The sort of pottering colonials
Who brought an end to British rule!
While you admired the Banyan trees

And looked out for sick animals,
We governed to a different tune . . ."
"Looks like old Rog has lost his cool."
"I call him a buffoon!"

"Sic him, Sister." "Zippy, how did you . . .?"
"We hooked up at the London Zoo:
Standing in the flamingo posture—
Do you do yoga, man?—
I had a vision of a town
Dissolving into cows and pasture,
And there she was. Jean's heavy, man, she's down."

I often think of Zippy's
Contradictions as my own:
Author of *Revolutionary Remnants*
("Zippy's what comes after Yippees"),
He turned from Politics to Art
As the best way to show his heart;
He too is a self-mocking clown.

Once we're above the polyglot
Confusion of the morning mists,
They vanish at the sun's high sign;
Now where an umbrella lists
Above a terrace basking in a plot
Cut from a stand of soughing pain,
We will find Marian.

III. "Life could be a dream . . ."

O brimming glass and heaping plate!
O lower case symposium:
A passionate, preposterous spate
Of topics burning as the sun,
High as the celebrants!

How is it lunches in Elysium
End no sooner than begun?

You'll know the feeling. Life recedes
Fast as the planet, plummeting
Beneath you at unearthly speeds,
Until it shows itself breathtakingly
Blue, beyond you; now, yearn
As you will, there is no return:
Anticipation's everything.

Once Zippy wanders off with Roxy,
Marian's elfin only child,
Little is left of lunch's wild
Claims and mild controversy;
Only Jean and your camera's zoom
Admire the sun's omniscient orthodoxy
And hear the chorus from "Sh-boom."

"Nice is a second childhood
When nothing adult intervenes
Between it and the first," Jean quips;
Then she assumes another avatar
As easily as she slips,
As I imagine, from her jeans
Skirt and eye-catching fishnet halter.

"The last I saw of my first husband,
He stood in Curzon Road non-plussed
At how the multi-colored Commonwealth
'Came home to roost in London';
All the done he'd have undone,
Beginning with the Hilton. On a lark
I walked away into Green Park."

Her stories seem to be set pieces,
A repertoire conceived
To spare her having to converse;
The vignettes frame a single thesis:
Life is simply to be lived.
"I dropped my scruples overboard
One night off Poros. I will not be bored."

Now in answer to my query:
"I'll not return to England yet;
I'm not yet ready for the weary
Tea-time tribunals life settles down to;
Travel suits me; I like the set
One meets in passing through;
I very much like you, "Enrico.'"

Here's Roxy on her Auntie's lap;
Would we like to hear a song
She learned before he took a nap?
Jumps down, disclosing Auntie's rare
Bronze thighs; runs off, "Ta-ta." A strong
Gust of wind fills the beach umbrella,
Straightens the pole, lifts it into the air.

A haze above the lake
Resolves into a towering thunderhead;
Jean has seen enough to suggest a
Retreat—I feel a cool toe snake
Its slow way from instep to knee—:
"I know where there's an extra bed.
Isn't it time for a siesta?"

It's time I felt less like a fool.
The young pines moan as the wind shifts,

And the umbrella just—collapses.
You can imagine Carmen, mistress
Of the impromptu rule
Of life—e.g., Live up to gifts
Or live it down—enjoying my distress.

If sex is so desirable,
If the magnetic other flushes us
Of pale particularity,
Filling us with the beguiling
Sense of a larger pattern, admirable
If unseen, then what pushes us
To resist feeling like a filing?

"Too smitten with my little sister?
You and the handyman.
He courts her with lewd proposition,
In dialect and pantomime,
Followed by comic opera contrition;
I can't imagine, knowing Marian,
Which is the greater waste of time."

Light strikes a table knife,
Then goes out; "Marian muddles through.
She *is* a mother; it's a life;
You're welcome to it, both of you!"
Winds howl, clouds race, rain splats; Jean rises, laughs
"You're both so . . . so . . . American!"
As she swept off, the storm swept in.

I like to think of Carmen as
An allopathic measure,
The surest antidote to Jean:
When all the world and the world's pleasure
Seem meaningless, demeaning, mean,

A dose of Carmen keeps me from contracting
The bitterness of interacting.

Skittish in company,
She's confident as queen or crone
In her stone studio alone
With her "things"—quirky odds and ends
Her presence shapes into mosaic.
Carmen's self-centeredness extends
To a worldview blissfully Ptolemaic.

"You know I'm fond of people, caro,
But not in person." "Carmen,
Coming from Marian's I saw Klaus' car . . ."
Evasion finds an ivory pipe
To finger, fidgets with a shawl:
"First, your dream. Klaus is not your type."
The firelight climbs an old stone wall.

The rainstorm gave way to the wind:
Tramontana flays the world,
Lays bare nerves. The lithe olive twigs,
Wrung into whirligigs,
Take on a lithic beauty as they grow;
But first we take a beating. Cold,
Earth braces for the three-day blow.

"High on the clerestory at Classe,
You, Jean, and Marian are crowned,
Gowned, gorgeous: three queens bearing coffers
Of stylized gold to the Pantocrator.
You reappear across
The brilliant nave—as kings!—with offers
Equally wanting, for God frowned."

Ivory on terra cotta tile
Shatters. Two lines down Carmen's face
Lengthen in flickerings of fire.
"You are the one who cannot smile
At what you've made of us. Your artifice
Slakes and awakes desire."
Winds fist the house; Carmen's eyes shine.

"Rising from the ashes of
Experience, desire
Flies to new likenesses of the one love
Forsaken, buried in the soul;
Love and its likenesses, divided
Like our natures by an aisle of fire,
Ask only that their poem be whole."

I can back up to backing out
From Marian's, under a cloud;
The rain let up as I wound down
To where the Saint smiled on the dripping town;
Taking the cemetery road
I saw the big white Jaguar,
Its thin black foreign *targa.*

The storm softened the bumps to lumps
In an old mattress. How I'd like a nap!
But here's Pampa, her face a map
To the traditional terrain
Of hard work, hard times, pain;
A chart too of an inner ocean
Gemmed with islands of devotion.

We share a wall in a stone farmhouse
Ringed by the olives, hills, and sky

Of paradise. She wants to talk
About the weather idol she swears by:
After the rain it turned to wine
Red, denoting a fine
Windy day, perfect for a walk.

Swept up in the broom-perfumed airs
The hillsides put on weeks ago,
I find myself at the old house I sense
Exists to show me how
To give in to the elements,
Stanza by abandoned stanza,
Until you know yourself as theirs.

The wind, as if it fed on cloud
Cleared from the heavens, strengthens, menaces:
Stumbling down the hill through scenes
Of staggering beauty, I feel the full
Thrust of the *tramontana* and, tired, fall
Through timeless terraces
Asleep to dream of Byzantines.

IV. In Summer's Wake

From here, an island in the middle
Of Trasimene in January,
In air as clear as memory,
What becomes of distance is a riddle:
There is the Summit wrapped in snow,
The "ugly town" thawing below,
Almost as near as in gray-green reflection.

—Recalling to a gray-green mind
"The old gray mirror": a weak line.
Sometimes reflection seems designed
To dwell on imperfection,

As though its helpless recollection
Were a reminder of divine
Admonishments that paradise is elsewhere.

But if from here, beyond the fall,
The *pomodoro* and the golden poem
Of summer may not have remained
So savory; if it seems the cost
Of knowing paradise at all
Is knowing it as lost,
Bliss exists to be regained.

From here I see our final fling
As clearly as I see the ferry's wake
Gradually widen, spread its arms
Until they take in everything,
Including summer's epigone;
Not that there's so much to take,
Just me, myself, alone.

Before our seasonal dispersion
We always come here for one last immersion
In late summer's faintly turned wine;
Today the stone streets hide
The restaurant in a maze of nets;
Everyone else must be inside;
For now the island is all mine.

As are the slippery path,
The cold stone benches leading to
A cell St. Francis filled with prayer.
For the saint, God is everywhere.
Right here, beside me, in the way the duck
Have of talking to the rock.
—I see what solitude can lead to.

Leads me to think the past survives
The seasons, willy-nilly thrives
In a kaleidoscope of images
Everywhere underfoot;
Tells me to look and I will find
The poem, in a turn of mind,
Fall into place as if each piece were put.

One piece will be the Christmas call
Collect, long-distance, Swiss,
From Klaus to the American;
By "playing ball" with the authorities,
He hopes to get them to unfreeze
His assets—as who doesn't! Please
Don't let milk and honey turn to cheese.

Another counts the unexplained
Loss of the housekey, left with Pampa
At summer's end, as so much gained:
Without it, what is there to do
But let imagination sow
Its crop of wild oats, strew
Its posies, though I hate to let it go.

We've always been belligerents:
"Your lack of confidence
In me, your self-doubt, is too dreary;
Call on your inner Journalist,
And do a documentary!"
Surrendering, I recognize its charm:
"What's missing, caro, is a tryst."

It will have Marian in a one-piece
Lavender bathing suit
Slipping away from the main course—

Lake eel baked in a piquant sauce—
To meet me near the Saint's crude likeness;
The other tourists, this hot day,
Imagination melts away.

Coming down the terra cotta path,
Glimpsed through fingers of summer's green
Like an elusive thought, caught as catch can,
I see maid Marian
("Roxy is a miracle
Of modern chemistry," chirped Jean),
Her face sun-burned—no, flushed with wrath.

"Did you imagine my seduction
Would please me, since it served your turn?
So little time, so much to learn!"
—So unpredictable, these powers.
"When you grow up, what do you want to be?"
I want what love would make of me.
"You might have brought me flowers."

So Protean a character, subdued,
Ought to prove oracular;
But I'm not really in the mood
For spirit-wrestling now;
I don't feel equal to the task
Of yet one more spectacular
Fall, *and* I don't know what to ask.

"You ought to try propitiation
Of a more ancient kind—like sacrifice."
What do you have in mind?
"Give up your cynical flirtation
With the self, and this cushy life;

The children must go too, the wife."
You're kidding. That's not very nice.

"You're not yet man enough for love
To make much of—look at yourself above
In your vague men: an understated
'American,' a blowhard Brit,
An adolescent bit
Of Sixties folklore, an adumbrated
Fugitive too featureless to focus."

My eye's drawn to the olive wood
Figure, standing open to the storm
Of elements—they've done it good:
In flourish, filigree, and furbelow,
The seasons stain its fraying habit;
Effects of wood rot form
The Saint's mouth into a shocked "O."

"You think your suffering
In a good cause or your inveterate
Nay-saying have made you a saint?
That deserves my sister's laughter!
If purity is what you're after,
Stop aping the illiterate
Expressions of the masses in spray paint."

She means to point me to the cell
Cut from a soft thin-layered shelf
Of sediment, the island's self,
Where the graffiti, passionately drawn,
Call art an impious scrawl,
Ego the writing on the wall.
But when I turn around, she's gone.

The stand of cypress, dark, erect,
Prompts me to straighten up, affect
Indifference to a loss of character,
Whose words struck so close to the bone
It seemed to be my own.
I don't know what to do or say.
Feeling the cold I walk away.

Part of the island hides behind
A high stone wall's glass-bristling cordon
Against the public eye;
Now if the island were all *mind,*
The gran' Palazzo, grounds, and garden—
Seen through an open gate!—would signify
The mansion of the gran' Unconscious.

Not that I'd think of going in
Even to follow Marian;
No more than, at the cemetery
Crowning the island, I can bury
My feeling for her words;
But sacrifice, except for *rarae aves*
Like St. Francis, is for the birds.

The ferry gives a hoot;
Tells me to come down to the dock
And watch the water, where the duck
Sit still, move, color, and reflect
Light playing on creation like a flute:
Beauty cannot be given up
But given into, stop by stop.

At home, late afternoon first chills
The air, chops olive wood, and lays a fire

In the heart-colored heating stove;
Then, admired from the porch,
Flames its way into a dark crotch
In the now palely blushing hills:
Who like the creator knows desire?

Silly, solemn, suicidal
With self-satisfaction—where, Love, are you?—
Summer's last act comes back to me:
I went next door to leave the key
And felt the season's mood
Changing, like Pampa's weather idol,
From rose to violet to blue.